Historical Sketch Of Hiram College, 1887

Hiram College

In the interest of creating a more extensive selection of rare historical book reprints, we have chosen to reproduce this title even though it may possibly have occasional imperfections such as missing and blurred pages, missing text, poor pictures, markings, dark backgrounds and other reproduction issues beyond our control. Because this work is culturally important, we have made it available as a part of our commitment to protecting, preserving and promoting the world's literature. Thank you for your understanding.

HISTORICAL SKETCH

—OF—

HIRAM COLLEGE,

—1887.—

GARRETTSVILLE, O.:
THE ITEM PRINTING AND PUBLISHING CO.,
1887.

HIRAM COLLEGE.

Hiram College is located at Hiram, Portage County, Ohio, three and one half miles from Garrettsville, on the N. Y. P. & O. Railroad, and two miles from Hiram Station. The following sketch of its history will be divided into appropriate heads.

I.—THE ECLECTIC INSTITUTE.

1.—*First Steps.*

This Institute, like so many other educational foundations, had its origin in a religious movement. Between 1820 and 1830 the body of Christians called THE DISCIPLES, sometimes simply CHRISTIANS, had its rise. As the body did not originate in any striking historical event, as a secession or an excision, but in general religious conditions, it is impossible to assign a definite date. From the first, this movement took a strong hold of the Western Reserve, where its following soon became large. As early as 1844-5, some of the Disciples of the Reserve began to feel that they needed an institution of learning under their immediate control; which feeling became general and grew into a confessed want. Nothing, however, was done to supply the want until the year 1849. In the intervening years there had been a thorough discussion of the subject, and a substantial unanimity had been reached; as is shown by the rapid progress made when once practical steps began to be taken. The first of these steps was taken by an informal meeting of representative men from several churches, held in Russell, Geauga County, June 12, 1849. The proposition to establish a school was unanimously approved, and the secretary of the meeting was instructed to call, in its name, a convention of Church delegates, at which the views of a larger number of people might be ascertained. Such a convention was held in Bloomfield, Trumbull County, in August of the same year, when the proposition was again approved, and a call issued for a second delegate convention, to be held in Ravenna in October. In Ravenna aims and plans were discussed. Some were in favor of establishing a college; others favored a school of high but not of collegiate rank. After discussion, the latter view prevailed, all the delegates acquiescing in the final decision. A third delegate convention, held in Aurora, November 7, located the school at Hiram. A fourth delegate meeting was held in Hiram, December 20, when a provisional board was elected and other necessary action taken. The Legislature, by special act, March 1, 1850, granted a charter. May 7 following, the Board of Trustees organized under this charter. The same summer, near but a little south of the crest of the watershed dividing the waters of the Lake from those of the Ohio, in the middle of an eight-acre enclosure that has since become one of the most beautiful campuses in the State, as it is by nature one of the most commanding, a substantial and commodious building, three stories high, with a front of eighty-four feet and a depth of sixty-four, was erected. In this building, November 27, 1850, the new school went into operation. It was called THE WESTERN RESERVE ECLECTIC INSTITUTE. Isaac Errett, then a pastor at Warren, now editor of "The Christian Standard," suggested the name. The leading promoters of the enterprise were nearly all members of the Disciple Church, fully one half being ministers. All of these were well known in Northern Ohio, and many of them had a much wider celebrity. Funds to purchase the grounds and build the building were obtained by individual and church subscriptions. There were no donors to the funds in such amounts as to entitle them to particular mention. The healthfulness of the locality, the morality and liberality of the community, and the existence there of a flourishing church, appear to have been the decisive considerations in locating the school at Hiram.

1.—Aims of the Institution.—The Charter.

The aims of the School were both general and special; more narrowly they were these :

(1) To provide a sound scientific and literary education.

(2) To temper and sweeten such education with moral and scriptural knowledge.

(3) To educate young men for the ministry.

One peculiar tenet of the religious movement in which it originated, was impressed upon the Eclectic Institute at its organization. The Disciples believed that the Bible had been in a degree obscured by theological speculations and ecclesiastical systems. Hence, they proposed a revolt from the theology of the schools, and made an overture to men to come face to face with the Scriptures. They believed, also, that to the Holy Writings belonged a larger place in general culture than had yet been accorded to them. Accordingly, in all their educational institutions they have emphasized the Bible and its relative branches of knowledge. The charter of the Eclectic Institute therefore declared the purpose of the institution to be : "The instruction of youth of both sexes in the various branches of literature and science, especially of moral science as based on the facts and precepts of the Holy Scriptures." What the special aim was, and how it has been realized, will be more fully stated under another head.

The Act of Incorporation consists of seven sections. The first created George Pow, Samuel Church, Aaron Davis, Isaac Errett, Carnot Mason, Zeb Rudolph, Symonds Ryder, J. A. Ford, Kimball Porter, William Hayden, Frederic Williams, and A. S. Hayden, a body corporate and politic, by the name and style of the Western Reserve Eclectic Institute, to be located in Hiram. It further invested these corporators with the power of perpetual succession, and limited the capital stock of the corporation to $50,000, to be divided into shares of $25.00 each, and to be used for no purpose other than education. Section second clothed the corporation with the usual powers in respect to buying, selling, and holding property. The third declared that the corporate concerns of said Institute should be managed by a Board of Trustees of not less than nine nor more than twelve men, any five of whom shall constitute a quorum ; and invested them with the power to fill vacancies, to appoint the customary Board officers, to select teachers, and to exercise a general management over the affairs of the institution. Section fourth provided that the President of the Board shall execute all contracts and seal them with the corporate seal. Section fifth provided for the election by the stockholders of a Board of Trustees as soon as $7,000 was subscribed to the capital stock, limiting the electoral power of the stockholders by this provision: "Provided that no stockholder shall have more than four votes for $100, six votes for $200, seven votes for $300, and eight votes for $400 or more." It provided, also, that no one should vote on stock not paid up. One third of the Board, after the first election, were to be elected each year. The sixth section provided for annual meetings of the stockholders to elect trustees, but said a failure to elect should not work the dissolution of the corporation. The last section gave the Board power to make by-laws for the government of the institution, and to prescribe the mode of transferring the stock.

3.—*The Eclectic Institute at Work.*

The Board of Trustees, July 17, 1850, chose Rev. A. S. Hayden, a preacher of culture, who had been connected with all the preliminary movements, Principal of the Institute. His principal associate in the faculty, at first, was Thomas Munnell, an alumnus of Bethany College, since more widely known as a preacher in Kentucky. More help being needed, Mr. C. D. Wilber, since well known in the West as a geologist, and Miss Almeda A. Booth, long well known in Ohio as an elegant scholar and an accomplished teacher, were called to the assistance of Mr. Hayden and Mr. Munnell. In the fall of 1850, Mr. Norman Dunshee, an alumnus of Western Reserve College, now Professor of Mathematics in Oskaloosa College, Iowa, was called in. Changes in the corps of instructors were somewhat frequent. In the catalogue for the year 1852–3, appear the names of Amaziah Hull, now Professor of Languages in Oskaloosa College, and J. A. Garfield. S. S. Hillier, an attorney in New York, appears in two or three early catalogues. A little later, the names of H. W. Everest, now President of Garfield University, Wichita, Kansas, and J. H. Rhodes, now an attorney in Cleveland, both prominent teachers, appear. Instructors who served for a brief period or in subordinate positions, are passed by for want of space. J. W. Lusk and the Spencers, father and sons, were for many years employed as teachers of penmanship. The learned T. E. Suliot served as an instructor for a time. In 1857, Mr. Hayden resigned the

HISTORICAL SKETCH OF HIRAM COLLEGE.

Principalship, and was succeeded by J. A. Garfield. The institution, which had been very prosperous under Mr. Hayden's administration, now reached a still higher degree of prosperity. Mr. Garfield won a wide popularity as a teacher, manager, and lecturer on general and scientific topics. His active connection with the School ceased in 1861, though his name remained on the catalogue as acting or advising Principal three or four years longer. From 1861 to the organization of the college, there were frequent changes in the head of the School. H. W. Everest, C. W. Heywood, A. J. Thomson, and J. M. Atwater served for brief periods. After the school was fairly under way, most of the teachers were chosed from among those who had studied within its walls. Some of the instructors took high rank as teachers; a smaller number, a higher rank in other callings. The tuition receipts were the only funds available to pay instructors. As might be supposed, salaries were so small as to be almost insignificant, and teaching was a labor of love. This fact goes a good ways towards explaining the frequent changes. At the same time, all of the most prominent teachers remained a number of years, becoming completely identified with the school and doing an amount of excellent teaching in the spirit of self-sacrifice that has never been properly appreciated but by the few.

The institution rose at once to a high degree of popularity. On the opening day, eighty-four students were in attendance, and soon the number rose to two or three hundred per term. Students came from a wide region of country. Ohio furnished the larger number, but there was a liberal patronage from Canada, New York, and Pennsylvania; a considerable number came from the South, and a still larger number from the West. These students differed widely in age, ability, culture, and wants. Some received Grammar School instruction; others High School instruction; while others still pushed on far into the regular College course. Classes were organized and taught in the collegiate studies as they were called for. No degrees were conferred, and no students were graduated. After they had mastered the English studies, students were allowed a wide range of choice. The principle of election had free course. A course of study was published in the catalogue after the first year or two; but it was rather a list of studies taught as they were called for than a cirriculum that students pretended closely to follow. Leave is taken of the Eclectic Institute with the remark, that it soon won and for many years held a first place among Ohio schools of similar rank.

II.—HIRAM COLLEGE.

1.—Organization.

In the first part of this sketch, it has been stated that some of the founders of the institution were in favor of establishing a college in the beginning. The proposition to reorganize it as a college was considered from time to time, until the Board decided to take that step. The Board, February 20, 1867, changed the name of the Eclectic Institute, and clothed it with collegiate powers and responsibilities. As Hiram had become widely and favorably known as the seat of the Institute, the name now chosen was Hiram College. It was believed that this action would add to the usefulness and influence of the school, and that a stronger financial basis could be secured thereby. Both of these expectations have been met. June 19, 1872, the Board, in pursuance of the statute for such cases made and provided, increased the number of trustees to twenty-four. It should be added that a convention of friends of the institution, held in Hiram, June 12, 1867, endorsed the action by which it was made a college. The College began its work August 31, 1867.

The change in the name and rank of the institution did not essentially change its aims and spirit. The work formerly done has gone on all the same. It was the addition of a college to an academical and preparatory school. The announcement put forth in 1867 declared the aim of the College to be "to furnish a course of training as thorough as any in the country;" "to bestow careful attention upon the classical languages," and especially "to give a fuller course than is common in those branches which are modern and national."

2.—Instructors.

The first President of the College was Dr. Silas E. Shepard, A. M., now deceased. He resigned at the close of one year, and was succeeded by J. M. Atwater, A. M., now pastor of the Church of Christ at Ada, O. President Atwater resigned after two years service, and B. A. Hinsdale, A. M., was elected to the position in 1870. He had previously been a teacher in the

Eclectic Instititute, and had served one year in the College as Professor of History, Literature, and Political Science. Mr. Hinsdale continued to discharge the duties of President until the close of the college year 1882, and retained his nominal connection with the College until June, 1883. At the beginning of the college year 1882, B. S. Dean, pastor of the Church at Hiram, was elected Vice President of the College, and empowered to act as President for the year. At the annual meeting of the Board in June, 1883, G. H. Laughlin, A. M., who for some years previous had been President of Oskaloosa College, Iowa, was called to the presidency of Hiram. He entered upon his labors at the beginning of the following school year, and has served unto the present time.

The first Professor of Ancient Languages was J. M. Atwater, A. M. Becoming President, he was succeeded by his brother, Amzi Atwater, A. B., who served one year. The following year the chair was filled by J. C. Cannon, A. M., then for two years by I. N. Demmon, A. M., now Professor of English Literature in the University of Michigan. Grove E. Barber, A. M., succeeded him and served until 1881, when G. A. Peckham, A. M., the present incumbent, was elected. Professor Barber has since been elected to the chair of Latin in the University of Nebraska. The chair of Mathematics was at first combined with that of Modern Languages, and filled for two years by Asa M. Weston, A. M. In the third year of the College, Mathematics was taught by the President. Thence to 1875 the chair was filled by Wilson S. Atkinson, A. M., now deceased. Colman Bancroft, M. S., is the present incumbent. The first regular Professor of Natural Sciences was E. B. Wakefield, A. M., though E. A. Pardee, B. S., served as tutor in this department in the second and third years of the College. In 1873 Mr. Wakefield was succeeded by G. H. Colton, M. S., who still occupies the position. This chair has been endowed by Robert Kerr, of Marion, and the President's by the citizens of Hiram. No separate department of Modern Languages or of English Literature existed in the first year of the College. The work was done by the other teachers. Miss Mary B. Jewett, A. M., now Professor of English Literature in Buchtel College, was made Professor of the former in 1879, and A. C. Pierson, Ph. M., of the latter in 1882. Mr. Pierson still retains the position.

A. J. Squire, M. D. served the College eight years as Professor of Chemistry and Lecturer upon Physiology and Hygiene. O. C. Hill, A. M. was for a number of years Principal of the Commercial and Business Department. Among the many teachers of music, Mrs. J. C. Ellis has served the longest. Many others chosen mostly from among its students, have served the College in different capacities. The German Language was taught for several years by Mrs. Mary E. Hinsdale. The Lady Principals of the College have been Miss Lottie M. Sackett, Miss Cortintia C. Munson, Miss Juliette Cumstock, Miss Ellen Jackson, Mrs. Marietta Cuscaden, Mrs. P. B. Clapp, Miss Mary B. Jewett, Miss Minnie E. Robison, and Miss Kate I. Beattie.

3.—*Improvements.*

The year 1878 was marked by the building of the Tabernacle. For all ordinary public entertainments the College chapel was sufficient, but the Commencement exercises had been held under a large canvass tent erected on the grounds or in the neighborhood. The inconveniences attending this arrangement led to the discussion of the feasibility of erecting a building to meet the needs of the Commencement period. With the aid of the Board of Trustees, the Literary Societies, and the citizens of Hiram, such a building was erected, having a seating capacity of 1,200. The first exercises were held in it June 20th, 1878.

On the 11th of June, 1879, the Board, then in annual session at Hiram, received a petition signed by forty-five ladies of the village and vicinity. This petition, after setting forth the necessity for some larger and better provision for accommodating students, desired the Board to appropriate some part of the College funds to erect a boarding hall, and stated that if this were done, the petitioners would agree to furnish it with all the appliances necessary for its successful management. The proposition was carefully considered at this meeting, and a building committee appointed. Alvah Udall, Redington Stanhope, and J. J. Ryder constituted the committee. Further steps were taken at two subsequent special meetings. The property known as the Smith property on the north side of the campus was purchased, and upon it was erected a substantial brick boarding hall, which was thrown open to students in

December, 1879. The hall is arranged with sleeping apartments for ladies only, but accommodates both sexes with table board. The following year the large frame house that stood on the Smith property was fitted up for a gentlemen's hall. Partly to these improvements and partly to the labors of Rev. Alanson Wilcox, the Financial Agent appointed by the Board in 1879, is due the impetus received by the College in 1880. This impetus, to say the least, has been maintained up to the present time.

Beginning with the year 1882, several important changes were made in Hiram's course of study. At a meeting of the State College Association held at Denison University, Granville, O., in the last week of December, 1881, a resolution was adopted requiring all colleges that wished to retain membership in the Association, to make their courses of study equal in point of time and amount of work done. As a consequence of this action the Scientific course in Hiram's curriculum was dropped, the Latin and Scientific course was made a Philosophical, and studies enough added to it and the Classical to bring both up to the required level. In 1885 the Scientific course was re-established. Its requirements were made the same in point of time and amount of work as for each of the other two. The courses of study are now all six years long. In 1883 the Board established the Department of Biblical Literature. Vice President Dean was placed at its head the ensuing year. The course of study for this department first appears in the catalogue in 1884. In 1882 the Department of Art, which had been a feature of the institution in an earlier day, was revived and placed under the supervision of Mrs. Emma J. Dean.

4.—The Commencement of 1880.

The Commencement of 1880 was of unusual interest, owing to the presence of General James A. Garfield, who a few days before had been nominated for President of the United States. It was also the year for the regular meeting of the College Reunion Association. This meeting was held the day after Commencement, and was presided over by the distinguished man. The news of his election the ensuing fall was received with great joy in Hiram. On the 4th of February, 1881, he made his last visit to the village, when he made a short but touching address to the citizens and students in the

College chapel. It is safe to say that from no point on the Continent was the ebb and flow of his life, during the eleven long weeks of his sickness, watched more anxiously than from Hiram Hill. On the 24th of September a large body of College students and citizens attended the Hiram College Memorial Service in the 1st Presbyterian church at Cleveland.

III.—THE NEW COLLEGE BUILDING.
1.—*Needs and Plans.*

As time went on after the organization of the College, the need of more room began gradually to be felt. In the early days of the Eclectic Institute three Literary Societies had been founded: the Olive Branch in 1853; the Delphic in 1854; and the Hesperian in 1855. The libraries of these Societies, together with that of the College, rapidly increased. Recitation rooms had always served for society halls. Added to this the great advance made in late years in the field of the natural sciences demanded better facilities for teaching them than Hiram afforded. Rambling talk of a new building was heard at times, but the school was not financially strong, and the consummation of an end so much desired was thought to be far in the future. The need became more and more urgent. In his annual report for 1881, President Hinsdale thus presented the matter to the Board: "We urgently need more room; our libraries have outgrown their accommodations; we need a lecture room and a laboratory for the Scientific Department. Were it possible, a new building to contain a library, a laboratory, society halls, and a lecture room should be built at once." Vice President Dean brought the matter before the Board in his annual report for 1883, and President Laughlin did the same in 1884. President Hinsdale also issued a private circular to the members of the Board in 1882, in which he urged them to give expression to their views, at the approaching annual meeting, on the subject of a new building. On the 11th of February, 1884, a meeting of the Board was held at Cleveland, at which the principal subject of discussion was the needs of Hiram. A committee of three was appointed to draft a subscription paper to raise funds for the new building and for repairing the old one. At the annual meeting in June following the members of the College Faculty were authorized to aid in raising these funds. A canvass was immediately begun. Considerable progress was made, principally, however, through the labors of President Laughlin, and a favorable report made to the Board in 1885. The summer of this year saw the friends of the college awakening to a real sense of its needs. On the 17th of July a meeting was held in the College chapel. It resulted in the appointment of a committee of fifteen citizens of Hiram and adjoining townships, who were to take steps looking to a more thorough canvass, especially of Portage County. This committee met on the 30th of July. A subscription paper was drafted to raise funds to pay an agent for making the canvass. Rev. Orris Atwater was subsequently chosen at a nominal salary. Rev. B. S. Dean volunteered to canvass Hiram, and Mr. W. H. C. Newington was made a committee to solicit aid from the alumni.

By the following spring it was deemed that pledges sufficient had been taken to justify a beginning. On the 31st of March, 1886, a special meeting of the College Board was held in Garrettsville. The results of the canvass were presented, and the Board authorized the work of building to proceed. A building committee consisting of ten members was elected, and clothed with power to act. The following gentlemen constituted this committee, the first six being members of the Board of Trustees: Abram Teachout, Cleveland; Wm. Bowler, Cleveland; J. J. Ryder, Hiram; B. F. Waters, Hiram; Dr. I. A. Thayer, New Castle, Pa.; E. B. Wakefield, Warren; G. H. Colton, Hiram; F. A. Derthick, Mantua; James Norton, Garrettsville; D. H. Beaman, Hiram.

On the 16th of April the committee met at Hiram and organized. Abram Teachout was chosen chairman, and G. H. Colton, Sec. and Treas. Many plans were looked over for a separate building and for remodeling the old one. The plan finally adopted contemplated the latter. The architect who proposed it was S. W. Foulk, of New Castle, Pa. The roof of the old building was to be removed, an extension added to its front, and the whole structure raised another story. This plan was decided upon on the 8th of May. On the 21st of May the contract was awarded to C. W. and J. L. Weaver, of Sharon, Pa. Work was begun on the 8th of June. It was pushed so rapidly that the corner stone of the structure was laid on Commencement day, June 17th, with appropriate ceremonies.

A large concourse of people was present on the occasion. The traditional box containing papers, coins, etc., was deposited under the stone. Speeches were made by Dr. I. A. Thayer, B. J. Radford, and Wm. Bowler. Abram Teachout coucluded the exercises in an appropriate manner. The contract called for the completion by September 28th of so much of the building as would accommodate the regular classes, and the whole was to be completed by December 1st. A failure on the part of the brickmaker to furnish the brick in time delayed the work so that the carpenters did not get through until February 19, 1887. During the fall term of 1886, and the fore part of the winter term, the Town Hall, and the "Baker House" on the west side of the campus were utilized for college purposes. The first classes recited in the new building Jan. 12, 1887. On the 11th of January the structure was dedicated.

3.—The Dedication.

The day appointed for this ceremony was very cold, nevertheless a large audience assembled in the new chapel. The exercises were appointed for 1:45 P. M., and at this time President Laughlin called the people to order. Rev. B. S. Dean offered the opening prayer, after which the studends sang "Ho! Reapers of Life's Harvest." Professor G. H. Colton presented the financial statement of the Building Committee. Mr. Abram Teachout then made the following address :

TO THE TRUSTEES AND FRIENDS OF HIRAM COLLEGE;—

Ladies and gentlemen: This college has for many years been far behind her sister colleges of the State in accommodations for its teachers and students. The want has been referred to in the annual report of its president for several years. It has been seriously considered by the friends of the school. Many valuable students have been lost because of this want. The lack of means to make the necessary improvements has been the chief trouble. It is well known that Hiram College is the outgrowth of the great religious reformation of the nineteenth century which culminated in the organization of what is known as the Christian or Disciple Church. "Colleges and churches," said the great Alexander Campbell, "go hand in hand in the progress of Christian civilization." "The number of colleges and churches in any community," said he, "is the index and exponent of its Christian civilization and advancement. Colleges and schools of every rank are or ought to be founded upon some great principle in nature and in human society." As chairman of the building committee I think that I can safely say that our belief in the

HISTORICAL SKETCH OF HIRAM COLLEGE. 15

above sentiment has stimulated us to accept the heavy responsibility and undertake the work. We have got it where it is, and have invited you here to see what we have done. In behalf of the committee, I thank you for coming, so many of you, and hope you will not have occasion to regret having spent the day in Hiram. I leave the details and circumstances which called the trustees to meet at Garrettsville to consider the matter of expending $10,000 that had been subscribed for building purposes to some other speaker, and shall confine myself briefly to t ie work of the committee. Your building committee was appointed at that meeting. Its members were selected from the store, the farms, the machine shop, and lumber yard; also one from the College faculty, who was quickly made secretary and treasurer of the committee.

We were given power to collect the $10,000 subscribed, to employ a solicitor to continue the subscription, and to go ahead with the work provided that we would assume all responsibility, and not encroach upon the endowment fund, or incur any obligations the college would be required to pay. When that resolution was passed the members of the committee looked into each other's faces rather hesitatingly. But, never having had such honors conferred upon them before, after a few brief consultations, they concluded to accept and try their luck. There were eight of us, and we were permitted to add to our number as our judgment should dictate. At our second meeting we appointed Rev. E. B. Wakefield, of Warren, O., and Dr. I. A. Thayer, of New Castle, Pa., to act with us on the committee. They have been a help to us, for if they could not furnish much money, they could pray for us and our success, which we felt at times we very much needed. We at once invited plans and estimates for a new building, not to cost over $15,000. Three competent architects furnished plans, which were investigated thoroughly at a meeting held in Hiram on the 27th of April. The plans were all good and the estimates reasonable, but they did not give the room needed. The old building was carefully looked over from basement to garret, with the idea of building the new in connection with the old so as to have all in one building, as more room and a better looking structure could thus be obtained for the money. It could be warmed with less expense, and would in every respect be more convenient. We therefore asked the competing architects to submit plans and estimates of that kind, which they did. We finally adopted the plans proposed by Mr. S. W. Foulk, of New Castle, Pa. Permit me to say here that there were great misgivings about altering or changing the old building so that its identity would in any way be lost. There was a unanimous feeling that, if practicable, it should stand upon Hiram Hill a monument of its thirty-six years' work and of the noble men who had occupied its presidential chair and are now numbered among the dead. The honorable and godly A. S. Hayden, the scholarly Dr. S. E. Shepard, the young, active, energetic teacher, brave soldier, distinguished statesman and martyred President, James A. Garfield; I take time to mention those that have finished their work and have gone to their reward. May not some enquiring mind of generations yet to come, in looking over the records of this institution and reading the life of the lamented Garfield and his connection with the history of our country from 1860 to the time of his death, look up to heaven and say :—

> "In those dark and stormy days of old
> Arose among the risings of his age,
> A man of massive and gigantic mold,
>   Whom we must measure as the Cretan sage
>   Measured the pyramids of ages past
>   By the far-reaching shadows which he cast.

Yes, my friends, the shadow of that wonderful man will reach far down into the ages. But I am digressing, and must return to my work. Your committee held three meetings at Garrettsville on May 15, 23, and 28, to open bids and consider and adopt a system of heating and ventilation. In the meantime Mr. Bowler and myself visited Oberlin and Toledo to get all the information we could in regard to the most improved system of heating. On the 29th day of May contract was made with C. W. Weaver, of Sharon, to erect the building, and with Isaac D. Smead & Co., of Toledo, for heating and ventilating. It became necessary to bargain for extras with Mr. Weaver from time to time, principally to make the old part of the building entirely new in all of its rooms. The work of excavating and quarrying the stone for the foundation was commenced on or about the 8th day of June, and the work was pushed as fast as possible. The corner stone was laid on the 17th of June, the day of the commencement exercises.

There has been general harmony in the committee. Some of them were thought to be a little slack about attending the called meetings, but when called to account for it gave us about the same satisfaction as the preacher received when he took his deacon to task for going to sleep every Sunday as soon as he had commenced his sermon. The deacon's answer was, "My dear brother, I have perfect confidence in you, and when you get fairly started in your sermon I know everything will be going right anyhow." I shall not be detracting one syllable from the efficiency of any member of the committee when I say to you that Brother Wm. Bowler has been untiring in his efforts; has spent more time here than any other member of the committee; has watched with a critical eye the work in every department, and has, I think, made a lasting impression and acquaintance with nearly every workman on the job. He has our sincere thanks. You have heard the report of the secretary and treasurer. Every dollar of the money has passed through his hands, and when we consider his duties as teacher in the College, it is almost a marvel that we find his book and statement in so accurate a condition as they are. Our soliciting agents, O. C. Atwater and B. S. Dean, have been industrious and have succeeded as well as could be expected. We have, as the treasurer's report shows, incurred a debt for which we are personally responsible, but we believe you have got value received, and will, according to your ability, help us to liquidate it. The money we have borrowed is for a reasonable length of time, and at a low rate of interest, all of it drawing only 6 per cent. We have been kindly tendered more money at that rate of interest than we needed, so that we are flattered that our credit has not suffered, and if you help us out we believe you will be doing a good work.

We should labor for the good of our race. This would be a dark and cheerless world if we lived for ourselves alone. We should live for one another. We should bear that sacred love through life's journey for each other that kindred spirits feel above.

> It's the Savior's great requirement,
> It's the gospel's great command.
> We should seek its just fulfillment
> If we'd win the better land,
> Where the loved ones gone before us
> Crossed to Jordan's farther side,
> Sit in circles waiting for us,
> O'er the dark and troubled tide.

At the close of Mr. Teachout's remarks, Rev. Jabez Hall, of Cleveland, then delivered the principal address, of which this is an abstract:

Mingling my congratulations today with all that love this institution and its past, and looking forward with something of hope for a large increase of its usefulness, I am glad to note the preservation of the older portions of this building, that part of it which has sheltered the students and teachers of the "Old Eclectic Institute," and the later "Hiram College." To you who have been part of this institution, and who owe to it more than you can ever pay back, more of mental and moral and, it may be, spiritual nourishment, and power to do good, to you the old is better than the new. If this is true of the more material structure, I hope it is not less true of that original thought and purpose which impelled the founders of Hiram Eclectic Institute to erect here an institution sacred to "Christian learning in which the Living Oracles—the word of God—should faithfully and fully be taught to all who should resort to this place for the purpose of being educated." Permit me then today to direct your thoughtful attention to the claims of this department of learning in this institution.

(1) Inasmuch as it was the principal thought of the founders of this college to make it a "School of the Bible," there rests upon us an obligation to foster this design. For we received this institution, thus planned and organized with this special character stamped upon it and wrought into its charter. The moneys contributed to the founding and perpetuating the institution were given for this purpose and with this end in view. The appeal urged constantly on the brotherhood of the "Disciples" has no other ground to stand on than this: that this institution is a school of the Bible, a Christian college. From the standpoint of obligation, then, we ought earnestly to strengthen and enlarge the department of Bible instruction in this institution.

(2) We ought to do this because it is a thing eminently fit and wise to do. Whatever views we may hold of the origin of the sacred books of the Christian religion, we cannot place them in a position much inferior to other literatures. The Bible, as a classic, is at least entitled to a prominent place among the best the world possesses. If the future shall not reverse the history of the past, the race will continue to draw from these fountains its richest nourishment for the life that now is. The knowledge it imparts can be gained from no other source; or from no other as well. Nor is any other knowledge so important to man as that given in the Bible. It has the promise of the life that now is, and of that which is to come.

How great is the debt of our modern literature to this one volume! The books that have sprung from it are, like the seed of Abraham, more for multitude than the stars. The great books, the enduring books, the vital books, have owed their best inspiration to its influence. Bunyan's Pilgrim's Progress and Milton's Paradise Lost owe not something but everything to the Sacred Book. It is commonly called "The Book"— "the Bible"—and well it may be, for it has no peer. Its vitality is only to be accounted for by its intrinsic excellence. As literature has no peer to this matchless "book of books," so it can have no substitute for it.

Whether we look at the historic, legislative, prophetic, poetic or didactic writings of the Bible, in each and every department we are met with unsurpassable excellences. Where is there such clearness, coupled with such terseness, as in the historic portions of Genesis; yet in these brief records we find the story of Joseph, which is perhaps "the finest example of narrative in literature"; and who can find a better "example of natural eloquence than the speech of Judah?" David strikes with matchless skill and power every chord of the human heart; and we feel today impelled to employ his very words to express our deepest experiences of joy and sorrow, faith and hope, penitence and prayer. Time will not suffice even to mention the excellencies of the Mosaic legislation, nor the influence it has exerted on all after times, nor the prophecies of the Old Testament, nor the portrayal of that absolutely perfect life which Jesus lived among men, the beauty of his teaching, the power of his gospel, the glory of his kingdom, the founding of his church, the instruction of apostles and the final visions of John. Nor need I pause before you to urge the question: Is it not a thing eminently fit and wise to make this book a special part of the study of every student in this Christian institution?

(3) Again, we ought to strengthen and enlarge the department of Bible instruction in this institution because we believe in it. The body of people known as "Disciples" have from the first placed special emphasis on Bible study. The college founded at Bethany, W. Va., by Alexander Campbell, made this its corner stone. In an address delivered at Bethany, May 31, 1858, on the laying of the corner stone of Bethany College, Wm. Campbell said: "From the origin of Bethany College, on the first Monday of November, 1841, till this day, a period of over sixteen years,

HISTORICAL SKETCH OF HIRAM COLLEGE. 19

there has been a Bible study, and a Bible lecture for every college day in the college year." * * * "In this corner stone we deposit a copy of the Holy Bible, not to bury it in the earth, but as a monumental symbol of the fact that this book, this everlasting document, ought to be the true and proper foundation of every literary, scientific, moral and religious institution—essential to the perfect and complete development of man in his whole constitution as a citizen of the commonwealth, a citizen of the kingdom of heaven, an heir of the universe through all the cycles of an eternal future." As a people we have abiding faith in these principles, and in this book. We believe that any education which is not molded by the teachings of the Bible, is so far defective. We believe that the Bible as a text-book should be studied every day in every one of our colleges, and that a student graduating from one of these institutions should know the Bible better than he knows any other book. Ought we not to conform our practice to our faith?

(4) We ought to give more, and more *thorough* attention to Bible instruction in *this* institution, because it is a crying need of the times. We want this institution to be abreast of the needs of the hour. There is no more urgent need at this time than that those who go forth from our colleges, to take as they will places of high responsibility and influence, should go panoplied in the armor of God, enriched with the knowledge of His will, acquainted with the teachings of His word. The influence of these teachings may be expected to affect the life and character of persons thus instructed for all time. Now it is lamentably true that the rising generation has but little valuable opportunity for acquiring Bible knowledge. Neither in the average home nor in the secular school is the Bible taught; and the church itself and the Sunday-school, though doing all they can under the present system, fall far short of supplying the deficiency. Where, then, shall this highest and best knowledge be acquired, if not in the Christian college? On account, therefore, of the pressing need, we ought to meet this demand. Let us respond to this need, and an appreciative people will send their sons and daughters, and churches will rally to the aid of this institution, and its work will be prospered.

Finally:—Numbers of young men come to this institution for the purpose of fitting themselves for the ministry of the word of God, and this number could easily be increased if the institution were fairly well equipped to give the requisite training. It surely needs no argument to prove that if this institution invites and encourages such persons to come here, it is under weighty obligations to furnish suitable instruction. That the institution has done something, nay, if it has done its best, it yet remains true that we owe it to these young men, the churches and homes sending them here, and to the cause which they are to represent, to enlarge and strengthen the department of Biblical instruction in this institution. May we not, then, appeal to all who love Hiram College, and especially to all who desire to see it doing a distinctive work as a Christian college, to use their influence and give their utmost aid to enable this institution to fully discharge its high duty in conforming to the original design of its founders, that the *Bible* may be taught, not speculations and dogmas whether orthodox or heterodox—but the Bible, its facts, precepts, promises, its moral and religious truth, its literature and its law. To do this, we must conserve the old—not less perchance of all that else is taught, but this, the complement of all the rest; that the whole man may be educated—body and soul—and so fully equipped for every good work in the world.

Mr. William Bowler, of Cleveland, followed in a speech of which the following is a summary:

LADIES AND GENTLEMEN:—As a friend of Hiram College, as a Trustee for several years, and possessing a good degree of faith, I have always believed firmly that the friends of the Institution would one day rally to its rescue and either give it a new building or thoroughly remodel the old one. I am sure that today we have good reason to rejoice over our future prospects. You will pardon me if I say to you that I feel somewhat elated at being one of the committee, through whose exertions this new building has been so nearly finished. At every annual meeting of the Trustees for years past, the subject of building has come up in some form or shape. Especially has there been great need of society halls: a need now happily provided for, and though I myself have never been a Delphic, a Hesperian or an Olivite, yet I now deem myself a member of them all. I am glad that such excellent provision has been made for the wants of these societies, and trust that the present students will be as much pleased with them as the old students will be surprised to see them.

Whether to remodel the old building, or to build a new one, or, indeed, to do both has been a serious question with the Building Committee. Sentiment moved many to oppose any change in the first building that would materially alter its appearance. Around it clung many sacred associations which such a change would naturally break up, so a separate building was the original idea of nearly all the committee. The plan finally decided upon you all know. I am glad to say that I have heard no one disapprove of it yet. Most every body seems to think that it was wise and prudent. Let me say to you now, that the first building has not been destroyed. The walls of the old Eclectic Institute are in this structure. Looking at it from the southwest, west, or northwest, the appearance of the brick will assure you of this. Even the former recitation rooms, though much improved in appearance, have not lost their identity. This chapel, in which you are comfortably seated, is still the same old chapel. True, it has been made ten feet longer, replastered, wainscotted and beautifully frescoed, otherwise it remains as of old. Perhaps I may add that the window casings have been replaced. I feel like taking it upon myself to thank Brother Abram Teachout, on behalf of the Building Committee and friends of the college, for his generous gift manifest in the improvements of this room. Among the relics of the old building which we have tried to preserve, you will find, in the basement, the stone frame of the front door and the threshhold worn almost thin by the feet that passed over it in the thirty-seven years of the old Hiram life.

You see for yourselves that the present building is much larger than the old one. The stories beginning with the basement are, respectively, eight, twelve, thirteen, and fourteen feet high. The tower is one hundred and thirteen feet high, and from the belfry a fine prospect of landscape and village can be commanded. We pride ourselves particularly, as a committee, in having secured one of the best possible systems of heating and ventilation.

In conclusion, ladies and gentlemen, permit me first to thank you for your attention, and second to express the hope that with the stimulus afforded by these new improvements, the future of Hiram College may continually grow brighter.

After Mr. Bowler's address short speeches were made by H. C. White and W. J. Ford, students of the old Eclectic, and by Elder E. B. Wakefield. Mr. Teachout then presented the new building to the Board of Trustees. J. H. Rhodes, as the representative of that body, accepted it with appropriate remarks, and committed it to the care of the Faculty. President Laughlin received the charge.

4.— Description.

The friends of the college assembled on this occasion were most agreeably surprised. The most sanguine among them had not looked for an edifice so elaborote and withal so roomy. That so good a one should be furnished at such small cost was a matter of remark. The original building at Hiram seems small compared with the one of which it is now a part. It was built in 1850 at a cost of about $7,000. It had a frontage, including the wings, of 84 feet, with a depth of 64 feet. There were two stories and a basement, and the height of the walls to the eaves was 41 feet. The wings were 22x24 feet. It was surmounted by a cupola 26½ feet high. The front of the present building is the same as that of the old. Its depth, however, is 103 feet. It is three stories high exclusive of the basement and its tower has an elevation of 113 feet. In the basement are found the furnaces, the celebrated Smead system of heating being in use. On the first floor is a large hall, at the end of which are the commercial room and the laboratory. On one side is the apparatus room and two large recitation rooms. Opposite these are three other recitation rooms. At the end of the hall in the second story is the chapel, large, airy, and beautifully frescoed. On this story also is found the library and reading rooms, together with four large recitation rooms. In the third story are the museum, the Y. M. C. A. rooms, and the three society rooms. These latter have been elegantly furnished at an expense of about $1,200. A large sky-light adds to the cheerfulness of the entrance hall. An important feature of the building is the method of heating it. The house was erected with a view of using the Smead system; the walls and floors are double, and so constructed as to give a continual circulation of air. Foul air is carried off at gratings placed near the floors in the walls, and pure warm or cold air can be let in by a simple mechanical contrivance. Thus the most perfect ventilation is secured. The cost of the building was about $21,000.

IV.—RESULTS—SUMMARY.

It is impossible to sum up in statistics the work of a school or other intellectual or moral agent. However, some approximation can be made in that way.

More than one hundred persons have taught at Hiram for longer or shorter periods. Counting up the footings in the annual catalogues, we have an aggregate of 12,006 students. Of different students there have been about 6,000. The average Hiram student has been enrolled in two annual catalogues; his attendance has been four terms. Since the Institute became a college, the attendance has been much more regular and these averages are much higher; still the preparatory classes, which are kept up as in the days of the Eclectic Institute, tend to keep the general average lower than it would otherwise be.

Geographically these students have been widely distributed. Of course, Ohio has furnished the great majority; but in the catalogues appear the names of twenty-four States, the District of Columbia, Canada, New Brunswick, Cuba, England and Germany. If the students furnished by the ten counties in Northern Ohio respectively should be separated from the mass, the number would be very impressive.

The aims originally set forth have been fully realized. Hiram was never intended to be a school of special training, and has never been a biblical or theological seminary. In all, more than one hundred ministers of the Gospel have been trained, in whole or in part, in Hiram. Special instruction in biblical studies has always been furnished to those desiring it. To these students the leading tenets of the Disciples have been taught, but all attempts to exercise over the body of students a peculiar denominational influence have been carefully avoided.

A large number of students have fitted themselves in Hiram for professional life. Notably is this true of school teachers. Many hundreds of excellent teachers have been sent to the army of educators. For thirty years a large number of schools—public, private and academical—have been manned by Hiram-trained teachers.

The total number of Alumni, including the present Senior class, is 109.

The original charter, which has never been changed in this particular, defines the object of the corporation to be "the instruction of youth of both sexes." In Hiram the experience of co-education has been successful. The education of youth is no doubt somewhat disturbed by what may be called the sexual differentiations, as most human activities are for that matter; but the disturbance is no more where they are thrown together in the same school than when they are taught apart. On the other hand, co-education is attended by some positive advantages.

With the new building, the institution whose history is given above, receives a new lease of life. It has survived a severe struggle with poverty. No other school in the State, it is believed, has put money to better advantage, or done more good work with the same cash expenditure. Such of its founders as have survived to this day, feel that their anticipations have been more than realized. They wrought under a religious impulse, but in no party or sect spirit. The thousands of students who have flocked to the school that they founded—coming from all churches and from no church—are the best proof of the spirit that these founders breathed into Hiram. Its first Principal, speaking of its planting, said a few years ago: "From this period the Institute has been before the eyes of the public, and its history is in the hearts of thousands of admiring students, who have from time to time enjoyed the benefits of its moral instruction and intellectual culture." These students, scattered over the whole Union, are found in every walk of life, doing their share of the work of American society. This honorable history of thirty-seven years is an element of power for the College's future work.

Printed by Libri Plureos GmbH in Hamburg, Germany